# NO LONGER SHY:
## CONQUERING SHYNESS AND SOCIAL ANXIETY

Reniel Anca

**Reniel Anca**

Copyright © Reniel Anca

All rights reserved.

No part of this book may be used or reproduced in any manner whatsoever without written permission, except in the case of brief quotations embodied in critical articles or reviews.

**ISBN:** 9798717352055

# Table of Contents

MY STORY .................................................................................. 1

Chapter 1 What Is Social Anxiety? ........................................ 5

Chapter 2 Overcome Your Insecurities and Unfounded Fears ....... 15

Chapter 3 Boost Your Self-Confidence and Self-Esteem ................. 29

Chapter 4 Be Mindful ............................................................ 41

Chapter 5 Try and Fail at New Things ................................. 47

Chapter 6 Allow Yourself to Be Vulnerable ........................ 51

Chapter 7 Finding Friends and Building New Connections ........... 53

Chapter 8 The Way Out into A New Vaster World ........... 59

NOTE TO READER ................................................................ 61

REFERENCES .......................................................................... 63

# MY STORY

I struggled with social anxiety and shyness like plenty of people do. For many years, I was crippled and trapped in a cycle of fears and worries. But I conquered my fears.

During puberty, I put on a lot of weight. I was bullied by other children for my weight which took a toll on my self-esteem. I dreaded looking at myself in the mirror; there were so many times that I felt so ugly and inadequate. I was an alien to a world that did not see nor understand me. It got to a point where, once, on my homework for values education, I drew myself and wrote that I wanted to lose weight so that people would stop calling me a 'pig'.

I was also impacted by the transition from a private school to a public high school. The private school gave me a sheltered childhood, and the public high school got me out of my private school bubble. I knew my parents could afford a private high school, but they chose to enroll me in a public school as they wanted me to become independent.

The change was so drastic that I found it very hard to cope with such a huge cultural shock, where I wouldn't have a dedicated pick-up and drop-off service and had to learn to commute on my own. I also had to sit in a class with almost 60 students compared to less than 30 in my previous school. I was not used to seeing so many students with different and dynamic personalities in the same room. This contributed to my shyness and social anxiety issues and further pushed me to erect walls of isolation.

Since I was shy, participating in any school activities was totally out of the question. But then, in my freshman year, my English teacher Mrs. Magalona asked me to do something that changed my life forever. She asked me to join her daughter who was in her final year and was forming a roster of candidates. Mrs. Magalona wanted me to run as a peace officer in the roster. I didn't want to join at first because I didn't think I had what it takes. But my mom pushed me to just go for it, and I took the leap of faith.

I had to go on stage and face my teachers and thousands of students to give a speech on why they should vote for me. It was really nerve-wracking for a shy and anxious kid to do that for the first time, but I made it through! And I'm glad I took that risk even though I didn't think I could do it. I ended up winning against my other 2 opponents.

After that experience, there was no stopping me. I learned to interact with different students and embraced my new life with my newfound confidence. Mrs. Magalona saw my potential, and I will always be grateful to her for her immense faith in me. And I didn't disappoint her.

I joined various school activities, including cheerleading, street dance, theatre, and jazz chant competitions. I also became a member of the school paper publication, contributing to the creation of a media that was informative and inspiring to students. In addition, I led and organized clubs and committees. For example, in my final year of high school, I was the president of the Youth for the Environment and Science Organization. Overall, I became a willing participant in what life had to offer and maximized my opportunities. My active lifestyle resulted in a transformative weight loss that elevated my confidence and self-esteem. I was no longer the overweight kid that was hiding in a corner. I became a better, stronger, and more attractive version of myself.

In high school, I eventually learned to try new things. I realized I just had to take a step! So, if you are fearful of taking a step and breaking out of your shell, I totally understand; I was there before. But you should take this vital first step (in fact, you already did by getting this book).

Freedom from shyness and social anxiety is very possible as long as you are willing to continue taking steps to victory. I was once trapped in a cocoon that I thought I could never escape from. When I was bullied, I thought there was no hope. However, one small experience gave me the courage to finally break through and transform into a more beautiful and empowered version of myself. You can too!

Just imagine being able to speak to anyone you want or give a presentation in front of a large audience. Imagine being able to pursue and capture the attention of the man or woman of your dreams. You no longer have to hide in social settings; instead, you can command attention and direct the flow of your conversations. You no longer have to be shy and obscure, or fade into the background. You can rise and put your unique stamp in the world. You can achieve your dreams and become the best version of yourself. This book will tell you how to get there. By the end, you will be armed with all the time-tested tools and strategies to build lasting confidence and eventually overcome social anxiety.

# Chapter 1

## What Is Social Anxiety?

In 2009, a nervous, painfully shy, and under-confident woman stepped on a stage and announced that she wanted to be a professional singer. She almost didn't do it, but she decided to pursue her dream. The audience laughed at her dowdy appearance and smirked at her announcement. But their laughs quickly melted to applause the moment she opened her mouth. An angelic voice rang out, captivating the attention of every attendee and flooring the judges. This woman could have never imagined what happened next. She became an overnight success and broke the internet, gaining fans in all corners of the world. At 47 years old, she was considered ordinary, extremely shy, and suffered from anxiety. But she was glad that she took the step that catapulted her to success, fame, and the fulfillment of her dream.

That woman is Susan Boyle, the woman that will forever define Britain's Got Talent.

Susan Boyle's background didn't seem to lead to a path of a professional singer. She was bullied as a child for being 'slow,' which led to under-confidence and anxiety. As an adult, she was diagnosed with Asperger's syndrome which explained her fear of social situations and introversion.

## The Differences Between Introversion, Shyness, And Social Anxiety

Boyle was not only shy but also suffered from social anxiety. This may not be the case with everyone. It is important to distinguish that you may be a shy introvert, but that doesn't mean that you have social anxiety. Some shy individuals may have social anxiety, but this is not the case for all. In fact, data reveals that social anxiety disorder is found in fewer than 25% of shy people!

So how can you know if you are socially anxious, shy, or both? As many of the signs are identical, it is easy to confuse shyness with social anxiety. Again, a shy person may not suffer from social anxiety, but shyness is usually not that very far behind. Specifically, shyness can emerge from time to time while social anxiety is a more permanent occurrence. In the Diagnostic and Statistical Manual of Mental Disorders (DSM-5), the noted diagnostic criteria designate it as lasting for six months or longer. Typically, the symptoms come up regularly.

Another significant difference is that self-criticism doesn't necessarily contribute to shyness. It is not generally seen as a bad trait by shy people who recognize it as merely part of who they are. However, people with social anxiety resent the hold that self-criticism has on them and blaming themselves for it. On the other hand, shyness may certainly induce nervous thoughts and actions, but it is natural; it is not a disordered pattern of thinking and diagnosis that interferes with one's quality of life.

**What Introversion is About**

Introversion is also a personality trait and is also distinct from both shyness and social anxiety. Shyness determines how you communicate socially, and introversion is about when and how people get their energy. For example, when introverts spend time alone, they are rejuvenated in contrast to extroverts that derive vitality by engaging with other people.

Social anxiety is most commonly faced by people who are shy. However, it can also affect extroverts and ambiverts. If you're introverted, you need to eliminate social stimulants to keep energized and satisfied, and you always get tired from socializing. An introvert may be happy to reject a party invitation, but anyone with social anxiety will feel disappointed in themselves, worried about what people would think about their absence.

**Social Anxiety is a Behavioral Illness**

Social anxiety signs are more severe than shy or introverted habits. Social anxiety brings about an excessive amount of apprehension, embarrassment, self-criticism, and self-consciousness in social settings. According to the Social Anxiety Institute, it is often known as Social Phobia. It is "a substantial degree of fear, shame or discomfort in social performance-based situations, to a point at which the afflicted person either avoids these circumstances or endures them with a high degree of distress."

It might sound scary to mark social anxiety as a mental illness. Still, it is formally defined in this manner by the DSM-5 (Diagnostic and Statistical Manual of Mental Disorders) of the American

Psychiatric Association. It is also the second-most reported type of anxiety. It is, in fact, more widespread than you would expect. When you've had it, how do you know? It is important not to focus on self-diagnosis but if you do pursue clinical help, there are clear things to look for to know.

It's important to note that if you have these signs, you're not alone and that things will get better. Work and focus are needed, but it's going to eventually pay off. If you suspect that you have social anxiety, consult with a professional to be sure.

**Social Anxiety vs. Introversion**

Introversion and social anxiety can look like a psychological 'potato, potahto'. So, how can you differentiate between the two? What's the bright line between an introverted disposition and confronting social fear? Let's look at four of the greatest differences:

1. **Introversion Is Inborn. Social Anxiety Is Developed.**

   Introversion, a from-the-womb, dyed-in-the-wool characteristic, is a part of the innate personality. And while those who are socially nervous still carry a hereditary predisposition for it, there is more at stake than mere temperament.

   Two things can make one socially anxious, the first of which is our performance. A person may conclude by experience that they do not measure up to those around them. For example, they may succumb to the fears of their parents, who are concerned about what their neighbors say. They may even be seized by trauma, like bullying, that leads to the belief that they are inadequate or lacking.

Avoidance is the second social anxiety ingredient. At the end of the conference, we bolt so that we skip the subsequent little chat, feign sickness so that we don't have to go to the holiday party or look at our phones anytime we feel anxious, all of which leaves us stuck. Moreover, we don't have the chance to figure out why this social stuff isn't as bad as we think it is.

2. **A Fear of Being Exposed Is a Part of Social Anxiety**

We think there's something wrong with us in terms of social anxiety. We have to know that our supposed defects are either not real or just true to a degree that no one cares about, even if we don't believe it.

The perceived weakness may be physical: maybe you think that you turn lobster-red when you talk or that your hands get sweaty while reciting a poem or something. Or it may be a character flaw when you think everyone assumes, you're dumb or a loser if you speak up in class. You may even be terrified of a bad social performance, like when you imagine yourself stunned and still, blinking in silent horror. No matter the alleged weakness, you're scared of exposure.

The non-socially insecure introvert, by comparison, assumes what you see is what you get. Nothing needs to be exposed, and nothing has to be covered.

3. **Perfectionism and All-or-Nothing Mentality**

   You presume you can either produce a perfect social success or end up on a YouTube reel dubbed "Epic Social Failures." This all-or-nothing mentality (no pressure or anything!) lets one feel that being clever and charming seamlessly is the best way to stave off imminent, harsh criticism. And that makes one feel paralyzed, in return.

   In comparison, for non-anxious introverts, being observed by others is not a problem because no verdict is expected. You can sprinkle your presentation with "ums", or have an uncomfortable silence in a conversation, and it would not mean anything negative about you, nor is anything at stake. In other words, certain conversations are easy to digest and flow. Others may be graceless or banal, but that doesn't mean you are too, you know.

4. **The Way Is Introversion. There's Social Anxiety Getting in The Way.**

   Social anxiety is triggered by dread. You may sneak away from birthday parties because you feel you're too bland to fit in. Another time you break out in hives at the thought of seeing a group of people.

   Sometimes you may even skip the cake and singing despite reassurances from your friends. Basically, social anxiety prevents you from living your life.

So, while social anxiety may sound like a souped-up form of introversion at first glance, they are as distinct as pad thai and pulled sliders of pork. The good news here? It will make all the difference in work, perspectives, and overcoming your fears. This anxiety is resolvable; you absolutely need not change any part of your introverted personality to work on it.

It is not fully known how each individual's personality comes into being. However, both the environment and biology are assumed to play a part, with new studies suggesting that the brains of introverts and extroverts react differently to interactions. It's important to remember that no one is exclusively an introvert or an extrovert; each of us includes at least a little bit of the other.

There are also ambiverts, those that are neither introverted nor extroverted predominantly. Introverts are mostly happy to be behind the scenes. Still, they are often present in even the most high-profile roles among business and political officials, journalists, musicians, entertainers, and even public speakers; using their prodigious forces of focus and introspection. When the situation calls for it, they can follow a more extroverted demeanor and recover in solitude.

**Consequences of Social Anxiety**

Childhood is the period when social skills grow and get ready for the struggles of puberty and adulthood. Kids who suffer from SAD (Social Anxiety Disorder) do not always develop socially acceptable habits. When children grow up with the condition, they can become used to social fears and build a life based on avoidance.

Having social anxiety disorder will have a detrimental effect on your education, career achievements, economic status, and intimate relationships. This can also lead to a lonely lifestyle or possibly addiction or substance abuse if things go out of hand. However, since this illness is treatable, people wait too long or never seek treatment. In reality, statistics indicate that about 70 percent of people with SAD can be treated with cognitive therapy effectively.

**General Anxiety Condition Screening**

To decide whether you follow the requirements for a diagnosis of SAD, the psychiatrist or mental health care provider will perform an in-depth interview. However, he or she can make you complete a screening measure as an intermediate step to assess the need for a more rigorous follow-up assessment.

The "Mini-SPIN" (Mini-Social Phobia Inventory) consisting of only three questions, is one such screening test. Dr. Jonathan Davidson, of the Department of Psychiatry, Duke University Medical Center, developed the Mini-SPIN (and its sister variant, the complete SPIN). Studies have shown that the Mini-SPIN is an essential method for diagnosing SAD among people of various cultures and languages.

Your psychiatrist will make you score the following three things on a scale of 0 to 4 to complete the SPIN in terms of how real they are to you, where 0 is "not at all," and four is "very current."

1. Fear of shame makes me stop doing stuff or talking to individuals.
2. I dislike operations in which I am the object of concern.
3. Among my worst fears are being humiliated or looking dumb.

Generally, overall ratings of 6 or higher are predictive of potential SAD, but a qualified mental health provider will only provide a decision dependent on a complete interview. There are some other tools, in addition to SPIN and Mini-SPIN, that can be used for social anxiety disorder screening, including:

- The Liebowitz Social Anxiety Scale (LSAS)
- The Fear of Negative Evaluation Scale (FNE scale)
- The Social Avoidance and Distress Scale (SADS)

While screening tools are very useful in detecting possible social anxiety disorders, a full diagnostic interview performed by a mental health provider is not replaceable. Your doctor will be able to offer a complete diagnosis or refer you to another specialist who is more knowledgeable in diagnosing the condition.

# Chapter 2

## Overcome Your Insecurities and Unfounded Fears

Almost 17 million American adults are estimated to meet the criteria for a social anxiety disorder or social phobia at some point. The percentage of people who suffer from shyness exceeds that number dramatically.

There are several successful strategies to, fortunately, conquer shyness and social anxiety and to build trust:

**1. Build Confidence**

Building confidence takes work, but it can be done. I know this because I was someone with a very low confidence. I couldn't even look someone in the eye in a conversation. Then one day, while speaking to my crush, I decided to take a step. I committed to making eye contact for at least 2 seconds. I counted 1,2 and breathed a sigh. It really wasn't that hard! Then I increased it to 4 seconds until I got better at it. After practicing this on a few more occasions, I now have no problems making eye contact. Mastering confidence comes from understanding and work. Remember that feeling when you first learned to ride a bicycle? At first, it was intimidating. But after you just went to get it and tried it, you got it, and you felt positive. Social trust works the same way.

Feeling nervous is not the issue; the issue is preventing social experiences. Get rid of fear, and nervousness can be resolved.

## 2. Engage

This includes taking part in small conversations at a checkout line and chatting at pubs, restaurants, malls, and the gym with a stranger or someone you find attractive. You can engage in small talk and ask them open-ended questions. However, don't forget to take a moment to observe them or your surroundings before approaching them. This is a great way to prepare yourself and give you a hint on how to strike up a conversation. In my case, I find it easier to connect with other people when I offer them a compliment first or ask for their names.

Don't be afraid to engage in casual talk and find something you have in common with people you find interesting. I have found that engaging with others can open up avenues to rich experiences and strengthen your connections. Remember to be polite and show your enthusiasm in hearing what they have to say; most people wouldn't mind answering a few questions from you or talking about themselves.

Keep in mind that life's so short. We are on the face of this planet for a short period of time, which is nothing compared to its age. Nobody remembers who was embarrassed or rejected 30 years ago so if you get rejected, who cares? As far as numbers are concerned, there are seven billion people in this world. How many can we expect to be like us? None! Nor can we be like any one of them.

So, grab any opportunity to initiate a conversation whenever you can and put yourself out there.

### 3. Try New Stuff

Join a club, an acting class, or a sports team. Select a new assignment, take on a tough job at work, or learn a new talent even if it makes you nervous. To get out of your comfort zone, you have to take that first small step and take that leap of faith, just like what I did when I ran for peace officer in my first year in high school. Back in the day, I didn't have any kind of experience as a classroom officer, let alone experience leading a bigger group of people and commanding their attention. But I still decided to put myself out there during my first few months in high school and faced the fear of the unknown because I had this "nothing to lose and everything to gain" mindset.

In some aspects of your life, part of overcoming shyness is about building trust and not letting anxiety, fear of disappointment, fear of rejection, or fear of embarrassment get in your way. You face the fear of the unknown by practicing new behaviors and trying new things that are way out of your comfort zone.

### 4. Talk

Start making presentations or speeches and sharing jokes or stories at any opportunity. Try to be more talkative, articulate, and engaging in all aspects of your life. You should practice communicating more freely; at work, with colleagues, strangers, or walking down the street. Let your voice and thoughts be heard. If you know the answer to a question during class or a group meeting, don't hesitate to confidently raise your hand and say what's on your mind or share your opinion about something related to the topic you are talking about.

There are instances in life when you need more explanation from people to understand what they meant though. In cases like this, it's okay to raise your hand, ask them to repeat what they said, and ask more questions to get more clarification. Sometimes you won't understand the topics discussed right away, and that's okay. Maybe you understood them to some extent, but you need to ask more questions to give you validation and reassurance. There's nothing wrong with that. Just do it, and don't be afraid to ask if it will help make you feel less anxious. I do it from time to time because I'd rather know that I'm on the same page with people than assume and hope that my level of understanding is right. Doing it this way will save you from a lot of trouble and conflict down the line.

Confident individuals are not worried about whether or not anyone would appreciate what they have to say. Since they want to communicate, interact, and connect with others, they speak their minds to understand and get things off their chest. This can be achieved if you don't hold yourself back from expressing yourself out of fear and shyness.

## 5. Open Yourself

I can tell you that being open is the best way to conquer this anxiety. If you're not used to this, practice doing this for those you can trust and are close to - like your mom or your best friend. Start with people already in your circle as I did with my close friends. I remember those fun times when they would ask me questions and act as if I'm being interviewed for a real job. I'm not going to lie; it was a little awkward at first because it was our first time doing something like that. It took us a while to finish our practice because we couldn't help but squeeze in some jokes and laughs here and there. I was proud because, in the end, we were able to push through.

Open yourself and let others see the real you. Be proud of who it is that you are and celebrate your scars and flaws. The more you do so, the closer you feel to someone, and the more satisfaction and significance you get out of those relationships. This would contribute to greater confidence in yourself and social skills as you go along.

### 6. Pay attention to your body language

When listening to someone, make eye contact. When you enter a room, keep your head up and greet people with a smile. From the smallest movement of your hands to the way you stand. Body language is a powerful form of nonverbal communication; understanding it will help improve your daily interactions.

When I was a kid, I was pretty studious and used to carry around a heavy bag full of books. I had bad posture because of this, and I didn't realize at that time that it was affecting my body negatively. I also had no clue that it was affecting other people's perception of me. Looking back, this situation made me think twice about how I present myself and made me realize how important it was to pay attention to my body language. Of course, this didn't happen overnight. I had to be patient with myself, and I focused on the areas that needed work. Self-awareness is key, especially if you want to be perceived positively by those around you.

**Social Anxiety Self-Help**

Self-help methods also rely on the productive elements of more conventional approaches to care. For instance, self-help could involve elements of calming, reprogramming of emotions, and exposure to dreaded scenarios. Here are some tips for you:

**1. Put yourself out there**

You might feel like you are in a rut most of the time if you suffer from mild to moderate social anxiety. The most effective way to break out of a rut is by doing something.

I'm quite a spontaneous person, and I like challenging myself from time to time. So, there are times when I accept invites to go to places, I've never visited before and do activities with friends that make me feel uneasy and uncomfortable, like watching horror movies. But you don't have to go to extreme or great lengths to make things happen. Sometimes we may get caught up believing that the improvements we need to make to get out of a rut need to be significant. You can just simply go talk to your new neighbors or volunteer in your local community and let people try your first ever baked goodies. By doing things you wouldn't normally do, you can understand, grow, mature, and improve who you are as a person.

## 2. Journaling

What I like about journaling is that you can confess your fears and struggles without punishment or any form of judgment. When I was struggling with self-confidence, one of the things that kept me going was getting all those negative thoughts and feelings that made me feel anxious out of my head and down on paper. Even if I only spent a short amount of time each day doing it, the world seemed clearer to me after I penned down my thoughts.

This is why I'm a huge fan of journaling. Taking the time to do this can help you understand your thoughts and feelings more clearly. It's a healthy way to express yourself, help you identify negative behaviors, recognize triggers/stressors, and learn ways to better manage and control those overwhelming emotions.

Chances are that your thoughts and emotions have become so ingrained that you do not even know what goes through your mind regularly. Slow down, take the time to reflect on the moment, and analyze the thoughts that run through your head, especially unpleasant ones.

For instance, "I'm so uncomfortable and humiliated", "the person I'm talking to thinks I'm strange", "they don't like me", "I dislike meeting new people", "I don't belong here", "I will never make a presentation at work", or "I'm never going to make new friends due to my fear".

Don't do this. Instead, tell yourself where the evidence for this conviction is. Consider if, from an analytical point of view, the perception of events is impractical. Are you using words that are exaggerated, like "never" or "always"? Are you taking reality or emotions into consideration?

Try to write from a different perspective.

For example:

"I assume, for starters, that I find myself strange and uncomfortable. But I don't know how I interpret the other guy. It is more probable that I confuse my emotions with reality."

Next, reframe your conviction to reconcile it with the tough assertion above. Render irrational thoughts logical by suppressing feelings and desires and substituting reality and probability for them.

"For one, I'm not going to come off as strange or uncomfortable. The barista/colleague/other passenger is presumably distracted and not even interested in my conversation, actions or response."

Reflect on what you write. What is it that you notice or feel? Make sure that the reframed sentences are checked so that they appear recognizable.

### 3. Enhance your fitness

If you're not exercising enough, start preparing a schedule today for yourself. Exercise not only increases feelings of wellbeing and lowers anxiety, but it provides the ability to build up your social skills in a comparatively non-threatening atmosphere if performed in the company of others.

There is also plenty you can do, even if you do not have the money or time to attend a gym or engage in daily fitness lessons. Consider cycling or biking at home or doing yoga and aerobics. You could also try to get a good workout and burn calories by climbing stairs. Going up the stairs can be a challenge, but each time I do it, I feel elated and relieved of stress. (Try it and see!).

## 4. Set goals

It's not enough to just wish and dream about a bright and promising future. It is important to set your aspirations down on paper too. Whether you wish to conquer the effects of social anxiety or become an Academy Award-winning actor, writing down your goals in life, or creating a vision board will help you keep your goals at the top of your mind and assist in visualization.

Deciding where you want to end up is part of target setting. But it also means learning and setting a benchmark for where you are now. One way to do this is to see how you score in terms of social anxiety by taking some self-assessment quizzes (the Liebowitz test is a decent one to try).

Then, down the line, you will do the quiz again after you have begun digging yourself out of the rut to see how your scores have changed. In terms of social performance, remember not to compare yourself to others; compare yourself to how you were doing one week, one month, or one year before.

## 5. Compliment yourself and become your best advocate

You may not be a strong public speaker, but there are plenty of things to be proud of in your life, like your time management skills or your innate creativity to make something out of nothing. Remember that you're facing struggles just like everyone else and that the little successes of your life can help you feel good. You may also feel proud some days that you've made it out of the door or your ability to wake up before your alarm clock. Recognize little milestones, and you are going to feel better about yourself.

Always remember that no one else will look out for you in the manner that you will look out for yourself. Don't be hard on yourself if you're having a bad day and things don't go your way.

When I'm down in the dumps, I usually say positive self-love affirmations. Some people do it in front of a mirror, but I usually do it in any quiet place where I say it as confidently as I can. To be honest, I used to be discouraged during my first few attempts with affirmations because I felt like I was just faking it, and it was doing nothing for me. But then I realized that I have to believe in what I'm doing because saying them is one thing but believing them is another.

Here are some of my favorite self-love affirmations:

- I matter.

- I am enough.

- Life does not have to be perfect to be great.

- Happiness is found within.
- My imperfections make me unique and special.
- I don't have to be anyone but myself.
- I was not made to give up.
- I embrace my unique individuality.
- I let go of negative self-talk.
- I am in control of my happiness.

It will feel uncomfortable at first, but I promise you that you'll get the hang of it. You can do it before bedtime or as soon as you wake up. It doesn't matter what time of the day or how many minutes you do it. What matters is the intention or your purpose behind it. You'll feel empowered if you give it your all and do it wholeheartedly.

## 6. Read good books

There is nothing in the world better than reading when it comes to enhancing the intellect and refreshing the soul. A book is always time and money well-spent. So needless to say, reading an inspiring book would help by giving you more positive outlooks. I love the way Kafka puts it – he considers a book to be an axe to break the frozen sea within us. There is no better metaphor than this. A good book will open an ocean of talent and possibilities within us.

Now in our case, an inspiring story, a self-help book, or a book on social anxiety would be great. Learn everything you can! The more you know, the lesser you need to fear. Get yourself learning more about social anxiety and how to get rid of it.

Read real-life stories of other people who were there; read motivational books about life. Now that you are trying everything that would give you newer perspectives and motivation, reading relevant books would open fresher, groundbreaking ideologies and philosophies that will help you along the journey.

**7. Avoid stalling**

Have you ever heard something more pointless than kicking the can down the road? Well, there is nothing more fruitless than procrastination. Perhaps you imagine a period in the future where you can overcome your fears. You may have more money to pay for treatment when you are older or feel better. But no one can be sure of what would happen the next moment, while you are also wasting each moment in hesitation.

This is also the actual problem with stalling upon a decision. You can easily confuse it with taking your time to start. The hesitation that is inherent to shyness and social anxiety can easily make you think that you are just thinking through and planning the execution of the decision. But the irony here is that there is never a better time than now for any new beginning.

Fact is, only when you actually step into something can it begin. So, stop procrastinating and start today on your path towards self-transformation. Don't wait until it's too late to become the best version of yourself. Try and figure out if you are actually stalling or planning. It's better late than never!

## 8. Reward yourself

Truth be told, the lack of encouragement is one of the causes of anxiety and shyness. You must remember not less than one instance where you had done something remarkable for your age or "perceived" character but was unappreciated. Didn't it feel disheartening? Did that not make you feel discouraged and the act itself worthless?

Such experiences and circumstances change a young mind's fundamental attitude towards achievement. Such discouragements get a person's spirit stuck in a rut.

This is why you should start appreciating and rewarding yourself for the simple achievements in life. Make yourself and your attainments be valued. If you never praise yourself for your work, it will not be any fun breaking out of the rut.

Treat yourself to something special, like a special dinner, a new book, a holiday with your closest pals, or some skincare products. This has worked incredibly for me to get my groove back.

You can bribe yourself into doing more this way. Just take care not to spoil yourself (or maybe, do spoil yourself). After all, you deserve it.

## 9. Ask for help

Under some circumstances and emergencies, social anxiety may go out of hand. You may feel extremely cornered or disconnected. Such situations are typical for us, but definitely not something to bear with. There is nothing to be ashamed or afraid of; you can and should get help when you need it.

Don't wait until you're in a crisis tomorrow, or next week, or the next time. Please make an appointment to meet someone today. You deserve the attention and care only compassionate, trained personnel can give you. You can ask a close friend or family member to accompany you or fix an appointment.

If you are not sure about calling a doctor, try contacting a mental health helpline in your country. Figure out what would be less daunting for you – speaking to someone you don't know at all or getting help from someone you know well. Find out what might work for you.

Simply take the first step.

# Chapter 3

## Boost Your Self-Confidence and Self-Esteem

Self-esteem, in a nutshell, is your view of yourself and your skills. It may be high, low, or somewhere in between. While everyone has concerns about themselves, low self-esteem will leave you feeling insecure and unmotivated at times. You might be able to recognize a few items that influence your own opinion - maybe you're getting bullied, perhaps you're feeling lonely, or it may be a mystery.

You'll be more likely to do new stuff because you believe in yourself. Trusting yourself is crucial to getting yourself out there - whether you apply for a promotion or sign up for a cooking class.

You are willing to commit your time to the job at hand because you are secure in yourself. It would help if you dedicated your attention to your efforts rather than wasting time and energy worrying that you aren't good enough. So, eventually, when you feel confident, you will do well.

For one, you'll concentrate on presenting your message to your audience if you feel positive about a presentation you're going to make. However, if you lack confidence in your abilities to speak, you will worry that no one is listening. You may fail to focus, and you may skip on your thoughts. This may strengthen your perception that your presentation is terrible.

Fortunately, there are things you can do to boost your self-confidence and help if you lack faith in one particular field or fail to feel optimistic about something. Here are 14 practical ways to easily enhance your self-esteem and to feel more secure:

**1. Avoid comparing yourself to others**

Comparisons are not safe, whether you compare your looks with your peers on Instagram or your paycheck to your friend's income. In reality, a Personality and Individual Differences study published in 2018 showed a strong correlation between jealousy and the way you feel about yourself.

Researchers observed that jealousy was experienced by persons who related themselves to others. And the more jealousy they had, the worse they felt for themselves. It can be a vicious loop.

Pay attention to occasions when your wealth, possessions, talents, successes, and qualities are compared. It would erode your faith in yourself and believe that other individuals are better or have more. If you notice that you are drawing comparisons, remind yourself that doing so is not helpful. All run a race of their own, and life isn't a contest.

Unfortunately, low self-esteem is a self-fulfilling prophecy. The more self-esteem you build, the more you can improve yourself because you know you're valuable. The lower the self-esteem, the lesser the incentives you pay yourself, and the lesser you can improve yourself.

It is a quick spiral down from there into a loop of pessimistic and circular thoughts, leaving you mired in harmful and mistaken beliefs.

How can you stop this vicious loop and start going in a more optimistic direction for yourself? Remember that it's a phase, and it's not going to happen immediately, but you can do stuff to get it started and keep it running.

## 2. Mastering a new skill

You increase your sense of competence as you become professional at something that fits your skills and desires. Imagine how you will feel if you are better at something than the people around you. You will be admired and respected for your knowledge. That will be a great confidence booster.

In my case, I knew ever since I was a young boy that I was good at writing, which is why I took up Communications in college. This course ignited my love and passion for writing and helped me discover many things about myself that I wasn't aware I was capable of. Of course, there were times when I would get frustrated for getting a "3 out of 10" for an article I wrote for hours or getting nominated for writing-related awards in school but never actually winning any. But that only made me more determined to do better next time and to improve on my craft even more.

Life is not always rainbows and butterflies. Sometimes, even if we put in all the work, we don't get what we want and what we think we deserve; and that's okay. I believe we have to experience all those disappointments, struggles, and frustrations in life to ignite that spark within us to keep learning, growing, and pushing ourselves until we gain enough knowledge and experience in a skill, we want to be great at.

## 3. Listing your achievements

We all have days when we feel extra insecure and anxious, but that doesn't make us less of a person. Emotions like these are part of human nature. During difficult days, it's hard to be positive; but this is also a time to be gentle to yourself and look for ways to make you feel better, like listing your achievements.

Think of all the good things that you have done and write them down. Create a list of everything you did that you were proud of and everything you did well. When you need a reminder of your capacity to get things done and do them well, check your list.

Aside from getting good grades in college and honing my interpersonal skills, another achievement on my list that puts a smile on my face every time I read it was when I won a competition called "The Noise." You're probably aware of the reality show "The Voice" where people with awesome singing voices compete. This competition was the opposite of that because people with bad singing voices got the chance to go on stage and let people hear their out-of-tune voices.

My college graduation was two months away at that time, and I told myself to just go for it because I wanted to do something out of my element. I have no regrets for doing something like that, even if others think that was a "cray-cray" thing to do. At the end of the day, what matters is that I was able to have a lot of fun doing it, and it also made a lot of people crack up. Even if it's not really a conventional type of achievement, it's something to be proud of for someone like me who grew up with a lot of confidence and social anxiety issues.

## 4. Do something creative

A perfect way to bring some beats and rhythm back into your life is by doing creative tasks. The brain is motivated by imagination; the more you do it, the bigger the gains. When you realize how much you can do and your ability to learn, you will easily become even more confident.

One of my favorites is to play charades with my friends because it eliminates talking, and people are forced to start thinking more creatively about how they can get their message across. Besides, learning new instruments, writing a story or poem, or signing up to produce a community theater are other fun activities that will encourage you to innovate and open up your mind to think out of the box.

## 5. Become specific on your principles

Everybody has their own set of ideologies, principles, inclinations, and sentiments. They are only stronger with people who had suffered from social awkwardness. To others, you are just an introvert; but deep down, you know your outlooks are nobler and stronger. For years, you have been the victim of several jabbing comments, but this might have only rendered your judgment, ethics, and integrity more impartial.

So, it is important to concrete these beliefs and morals before you set out on your new journey. Take a look at your life to see if you are able to meet your standards. If you are not living up to your expected levels, make the required changes. The better you outline what you stand for, the more confidently you will stand your ground.

## 6. Challenge your limits

Experiences don't just leave us with new habits and ethics; they leave deep imprints on our personality. When we're kids, we've not much control over the way that experiences influence us. But we need not let that happen anymore.

Your mind is your greatest asset, and it should be treasured. Stop yourself anytime you find your mind thinking poorly about yourself. Now, look at the achievements you have to your credit. Which have we learned to value more? Of course, it is our achievements.

So, the next step towards your progress is challenging the limits you've set on yourself. Don't let misleading thoughts limit you. Strive to find the roots of each negative thought that crosses your mind before letting it grip your peace or composure.

If the root cause is something that needs to be fixed, absolutely bring about that change! But please let it go if it is not worth your time or peace of mind. Remember to let go of any pointless thought that perturbs your mind.

## 7. Go far and beyond your comfort zone

Stepping out of your comfort zone is a leap much more powerful than we would assume. The comfort zone you've set for yourself is the most dangerous place to be. The comfort zone was created when your shyness and anxiety held you back from doing certain things. Now they have become more of a challenge, and the very same reserve keeps you from stepping out to do it. It is a vicious circle you need to break free from.

Robin Sharma's words present this idea I have perfectly: "As you move outside of your comfort zone, what was once the unknown and frightening becomes your new normal."

Persuade yourself to step to your comfort zone's edge. Get uncomfortable and try something new - meet different people, present yourself with new challenges, approach a situation that you wouldn't usually do. Change begins at the end of your comfort zone. So, dare to go far and beyond, and ultimately, you'll leave your comfort zone as far behind as you can.

## 8. Support somebody and become a mentor

As a writer and self-confidence coach, it's very important for me to encourage people to become the most confident version of themselves. I do this by:

- Using my strengths, knowledge, and experiences.
- Leading by example.

- Offering direct assistance, sharing useful information, or teaching what they want to understand.

You can do this too, by supporting someone in need of a helping hand and a shoulder to cry on whenever you can. Let them know they are not alone. Always remember that you don't need to do big things to change the world. The seemingly little things you do, like inspiring someone to take necessary actions to achieve their goals, showing them how to do things better, providing them a new perspective in their current situations, or listening to their problems with full attention, especially when they need it the most, could go a long way.

Helping a few people in need might not change the world entirely, but it could change their world. And when they show appreciation for the things you do for them, it has a profound effect on the way you think about yourself and helps you find more meaning in your life.

For anyone who wants your help, your leadership, and your encouragement, be there. Their respect and appreciation will contribute to your self-esteem and self-respect — and see them progress with your support.

9. **Heal your history**

Facing conflicts and crises is a fundamental part of life. You only know you are alive and are standing up to something when challenges come your way. But there is no reason to stay stuck in low self-esteem because of unresolved conflicts or drama.

Remember that every human being has a battle of their own and have seen many in the past. The battles and battering are what shapes an individual. But when you find it difficult to free yourself from the grip of your past mishaps, get help.

You need not forget them, nor do you need to still hurt from them. The key is healing the wounds your past has created in your mind and filling the voids with positivity. To help you heal, you may get the guidance of a professional psychologist.

There should be nothing in your way when you want to move on to the future in a confident and self-assured manner.

**10. Avoid trying to care about what people say**

The ugly truth is that people are going to think something!

Correction: people who have nothing better to do are going to think something.

The point is, you will never be able to be yourself if you care about what people will think of you. But then again, it is ironically pointless. Why would anyone's opinion matter to you? If a person is worth your worry, it should be someone you love. But the fact is that the people who love you already accept you the way you are and love every aspect of your being.

So, you need to make a strong commitment to cease worrying about what others might think. Follow the advice of Dr. Seuss and be who you are and say what you feel, because those who mind don't matter, and those who matter don't mind.

**11. Let go of pessimistic people**

People's opinions and attitudes may have a plethora of reasons. But that barely means you have to put up with everything. If there are negative people in your life, you will feel drained and exhausted more often. They may have nothing good to say, may be putting you down, or could be taking advantage of your introversion.

Letting go of such people and influence is the right thing to do. Of course, you should try and make them think more positively. But if it is difficult to cheer them up, you need not take their lot off on you.

The best way to find self-esteem is to associate yourself with optimistic, compassionate individuals who can respect and appreciate other people. Such people would change your life and perspective for good.

**12. Draw a line**

Any person has the right to some personal space and privacy. Being slightly on the introverted side, you may value it even more. But because people keep commenting on the cocoon, they see around you, you may feel inclined to let down your guard, especially as a teen.

And the results are almost immediate. You start having a bad feeling almost instantly, get regretful, and build even stronger, higher walls – which is completely avoidable.

Start by defining your personal limits. Once you know what is right for you and what is not, you can better understand your self-esteem. Know what your boundaries are, and when people cross them, be strong. This may sound rude, but it is not. It is only uncourteous if you can't be polite about it. Basically, don't let someone dominate you, bully you, or take advantage of you.

Set down ground rules and healthy limits and stick to them. You don't need to tell anyone about them; just watch if a person can naturally respect them. If a person tends to disregard their limits frequently, you can simply make yourself more comfortable and pull away a bit.

## 13. Accepting failures as a part of growth

You failed only because you tried something – it's as simple as that. Bear in mind that failure still means you are making an effort. If Thomas Alva Edison had given up any one of those 999 times, we would not have had the light bulb on his thousandth attempt!

It is very normal for us to be disheartened by failure. But being harsh on yourself is not the right way. You need not be discouraged either, like everyone.

When you lost at something, did you not find a way that absolutely does not work? Would you ever try that again?

This is the way out - using the failure to learn, changing your thinking, and realizing that loss is a chance to improve. When you always use your mistakes to step one level upward, you get new perspectives in learning and development.

## 14. Be a student

The ultimate mantra to conquering shyness, success, or anything in the world, for that matter, is learning. With newer ideas, perspectives, philosophies, and thoughts, along with deep contemplation on every one of those aspects, you give your attitude and perception a surge of rejuvenation.

Once you unlock the power of learning, you begin to think of yourself as a lifetime learner. This approach is what Zen Buddhism calls *Shoshin* or "beginner's mind". This is an attitude that helps you to approach anything you do with a student's mindset. And if you are ready to see the true potential of it, it is a lifestyle choice that provides nothing short of success in every one of your endeavors.

*Shoshin* prompts us to learn something like a beginner would; open, ready, impartial, unprejudiced, and more able to learn.

### Drawing strength from these techniques

These 14 ways to better self-esteem and confidence are not mere ingredients that would just make up a formula or course of action; they are each a source of power too. The moment you decide you want to do something that would make you value yourself more, you are on your way to empowerment.

Each moment you strive strictly towards a more revered and cherished you, you draw strength from the action itself. There is no chance for failure here. It is going to be a self-sustained process.

# Chapter 4

## Be Mindful

We do not belong in the past nor the future; we belong in the present. Life is exclusively accessible in the here and now, and this is actually where we should be.

Mindfulness is the energy that causes us to perceive the states of satisfaction that are now present in our lives. You don't need to wait for a long time to attain this satisfaction. It is available in each snapshot of your everyday life. There are some of us who are alive in all physical senses, yet do not relate much with that fact. When you gape into and try to know about your inner self, you will discover the larger marvel of being alive. That is the reason why mindfulness is a wellspring of satisfaction and bliss.

The vast majority of people who go on about their daily lives are distracted; they are not generally present most of the time. Their brains are trapped in their concerns, feelings of dread, outrage, and second thoughts and thus are not aware of what's happening around them. This condition is called distraction — you are physically present, yet your thoughts are elsewhere. You are trapped either in the past or in some version of the future. You are not there right now, carrying on with your life with neglect.

Something contrary to neglect is awareness. Awareness or mindfulness is the point at which you are genuinely there - brain and body together. Breathe in and out carefully and take your mind back into the present. At that point, you can perceive the numerous states of satisfaction that are inside and around.

## Become Aware and Mindful of Yourself and Your Surroundings

Rehearsing awareness is simple. Tune into your environmental factors and watch. How does your body feel? Would you be able to feel the contact between your feet and the floor, or your legs and the seat you are perched on? Feel your breath entering and leaving through your nose. Would you be able to hear anything? What would you be able to smell? Connect further to the energy in the room. How does it feel?

Do you need to put forth a conscious attempt to breathe in? It is not complicated. Simply take a breath. Assume you are at a gathering of individuals watching the sunset. Do you need to try so hard to appreciate the transformation of day into night? Nope. You don't need to do anything but watch and let it happen.

The next time you see a beautiful flower, focus on it and take the time to notice the details. Notice the color, shape, and form. When you are completely aware of the flower, you will get an opportunity to make a discovery about all its parts. This is what awareness will do; it will help you accomplish a deeper understanding and comprehension of yourself and enrich your present moments.

While you are remaining genuinely mindful, you will probably experience interruptions. Treat them as foundation commotions.

Try not to quiet the musings; instead, pull your attention together on the actual sensations you are experiencing.

## Understanding Your Non-Verbal Communication and Showing Certainty

Tension triggers many physiological responses in your body, prompting actual signs of dread, including a pounding heart, sweating, blushing red, shivering, and ending up with a dry mouth. You start to feel feeble, humiliated, and vulnerable in some situations

Changing your stance can profoundly affect your comfort levels and certainty. A great stance flags the brain to pump more hormones like testosterone and bring down cortisol levels. The impact is a vibe of intensity and confidence.

**To Harness the Force Within You**

1. Stand upright, hold your chin up, and pin your shoulders back. You should put your feet in a wide position and your hands on your hips or behind your head.

2. Keep up this position for two to five minutes preceding social situations, and you will be astonished at how sure you feel.

3. Be aware of your stance going forward.

Fundamental changes, for example, the position of strength, can redesign your social communications. Modest individuals will, in general, show their distress through obvious practices. Ladies typically gesture and smile excessively, while shy men will try to reduce the rate of eye contact. Be mindful of these telltale signs so that you can convey your solace and certainty to other people.

**The Right Way to Relax**

The breath is a great device for managing one's enthusiastic state. When restless contemplations take you over in a social setting, let the negativity leave your body through your breath.

You can likewise utilize your breath to try to avoid panicking in distressing social circumstances. Diaphragmatic breathing includes breathing profoundly into your stomach. While shallow breaths through the chest can make you feel more nervous or anxious, breathing into the belly helps you relax and lowers the dangerous effects of the stress hormone 'cortisol' on your body. Practice this breathing at home until you get the hang of it.

A transformation of this kind of breathing can be utilized to manage anxiety. Deep diaphragmatic breathing animates your body's parasympathetic or unwinding reaction. Inhale through your nose and fill your gut with air before it arrives at your upper lungs. Hold this breath for three seconds. Gradually discharge the air through a barely opened mouth while guaranteeing that your face and chest area stays loose. This will assist you in relieving any strain at the time and do so rapidly and naturally.

**How Mindfulness Has Transformed My Life**

When I was first acquainted with the concepts of mindfulness and awareness, I was rather intrigued. I too wondered how something so simple can help me with my social situation.

I even found it a bit odd, because I was already super-conscious about every aspect of myself. I wondered why I should adopt mindfulness after all. But I still decided to learn and approach the concept because of *Shoshin*.

Needless to say, I was dumbfounded by the kaleidoscope of possibilities that opened to me once I gave mindfulness a chance. I began seeing everything in a new light, in great details, and in its full depth. I began realizing that there is so much more to the trivial chores we perform every day.

From the blades of grass to skyscrapers, everything left me in awe. This is why I considered dedicating so much time to share with you my experience with mindfulness. From what I have experienced, it is one of the most powerful but underrated techniques in attaining your goals.

# Chapter 5

## Try and Fail at New Things

Social uneasiness can be a genuine hindrance to encountering life.

What's the main thing that enters your thoughts when you hear "disappointment"? An extensive rundown of negative descriptors? That is because the general public sees disappointments with such an opposing point of view that proposing it as something to be thankful for appears to be unusual. We revile ourselves for our disappointments and cry over our slip-ups. However, how often do we consider failures as opportunities to learn?

No one is perfect in this world. As people, we are bound to commit errors and that's okay. Remember that we can't figure out how to walk without falling. So, every time you fall, get yourself up and give it another try – that is the thing that successful people do!

Trying new things takes out two targets with one shot. Initially, you will pick up the occasion to encounter new conditions, individuals, and difficulties. Furthermore, you will assemble your certainty, making the new thing simpler later on.

**Discover Your Edge**

Your edge is the spot where you begin feeling awkward. Frequently, this spot is further away than you might suspect.

You should change your thinking at the slope of your edge and change your conduct to move past it.

Where is your edge? Inspect your ongoing social communications and locate any common trends. Do you quit connecting if the gathering expands? Do you feel overpowered when you are being posed questions?

In a social setting, try to provoke yourself to arrive at this goal line of distress. Push somewhat harder and move past it. Don't hesitate to go somewhat farther next time.

An example of this is by starting a discussion. Try to connect with somebody and attempt to start the discussion before they do. You will feel less questionable and less on edge if you are posing inquiries, raising the subjects, and coordinating the discussion instead of being asked questions and being approached first.

**Coming to Terms with Your Disappointments and Failures**

There's no denying that disappointments are a certain part of life. When you come out of your shell and try something wholly new, you are bound to come face to face with failures too. It is only natural. But only the one who does not flinch in the face of failures can succeed.

Try and remember that anyone succeeds in getting something right for the first time only once, after several failed attempts. The sentence may sound ridiculous, but come to think of it, we fell a thousand times as a toddler before our first step. Even the most brilliant scientists had thousands of attempts just to put through an idea they know on paper.

So the key is not letting yourself be put off when you need time to find success with something. The first time you try to pluck up the courage to try your hand at something, gather some courage to keep your spirits throughout the process. "I will not stop until I see success", would make an excellent mantra for you at any point. In a while, it will become as natural as the very air you breathe.

# Chapter 6

## Allow Yourself to Be Vulnerable

Being vulnerable and letting your walls down is actually not a bad thing. However, showing your vulnerability at times can be dangerous to a certain extent since you may be misconstrued, detested, or even dismissed. Yet the advantages exceed the dangers since it will be much simpler to associate yourself with others, especially if they can feel in their gut that you're being genuine.

We are social animals. While the majority of us think we need close associations, we oppose being vulnerable, the very characteristic that makes that association conceivable. In a culture that regularly applauds having toughness, and remaining strong and independent, we erroneously misunderstand being vulnerable as powerless. We trust it will unnecessarily open us to damages and humiliations we could undoubtedly stay away from. However, what vulnerability is truly about is simply the ability to uncover a gentler side of ourselves that isn't taking cover behind our safeguards. As specialist Brene Brown put it, "Vulnerability is tied in with having the fearlessness to appear and be seen."

You can rehearse vulnerability simply by attempting new things, being straightforward with individuals in your day-to-day life, requesting help, and opening up to other people who are interested. You can also take a shot at vulnerability through self-entertainment, which includes doing what you want to do and seeing what occurs. For instance, imagine that you're at a shopping center and you notice a piano accessible for public use. You can't help but take a closer look because you cherished piano lessons as a child. The self-delight attitude urges you to simply do it and doing so will make you happy – it's as simple as that.

In the same way, every single new attempt will end up in a surge of happiness if you either do what you love, or love what you do. If you think a task is daunting, boring, or time-consuming, pick out the elements in it that would engage your attention on some level or at some point. You can now complete the less engrossing elements with a reward in mind because there are some things that you like to do.

This technique would work even better if you teach your mind to feel happier when you get something done. This works wonders for me all the time. Since I have always enjoyed the pure bliss of satisfaction when I get something done, I am able to give any task my full enthusiasm, no matter how boring or difficult it is.

This can work wonderfully well in fighting anxiety too. The simple thought of opening new possibilities should be your reward in this process. Remember that you can always reach out to your loved ones for help when you are stepping into new arenas.

# Chapter 7

## Finding Friends and Building New Connections

If you are an introvert or a shy person, do not think that you are alone. The world is full of shy and awkward people; some stay that way through life, some build a different persona for others while intrinsically remaining the same, and others break the shackles of the cocoon of shyness to emerge as a gorgeous butterfly.

It is important to note that shyness is the result of both nature and nurture. People who are genetically inclined to be shy and introverted may find it more difficult to overcome it and become a part of the social settings. People who have grown up isolated, in a cyber-world, or away from contact with real people may be able to free themselves of shyness after changing their surroundings and environment.

Whatever the cause - genetics or upbringing, anything is possible if you want to make it possible. The same is the case with conquering shyness, finding new friends, and building new connections, in the online world as well as in the physical world.

Here are some of the thoughts and processes that assisted me in overcoming the odds imposed on me by my shyness, and I recommend that you apply them to help you live a more fulfilling life:

1. **Why do you want to make friends and build new connections?**

This is one of the most important questions that you have to understand, ponder, and answer honestly. Do you want to make friends because you are lonely; or to surround yourself with people; or to fill some gap that is missing in your life; or for some other reason? Or, do you want to build connections to get to know the world better; or meet new people and cultures and ideas; or move on to a better future?

It is vital to remember that choosing to become more expressive in social gatherings should not be born out of negativity, but out of a need to reach your goals and ambitions.

Thus, trying to make new friends just to get rid of your loneliness may not work out in the end because you may end up imposing yourself on others who may not be interested. When the underlying reason for building new connections is positive (such as getting to know new cultures, etc.), then you will by default listen more and talk less at first. Listening, which does come quite easily, helps us understand the viewpoints of others. Process their thoughts and conclude whether you can work with them. If yes, you can delve into the conversations and become a part of them, thereby becoming a wholesome part of the new group of friends.

If their viewpoints are poles apart from you and do not align with your general ideology of life, then it is best to move on. Forcing yourself into a group will only result in you being unhappy. The best option is to move on and keep trying to find new friends who are more compatible, and thus have a greater tendency to be lifelong companions.

## 2. Be at peace with yourself before commencing the search

It is essential to be at peace with oneself and to accept the person that you are before you try to solve other crises in your life. You can do yoga, exercise, eat right, meditate, etc., to become more confident, increase self-esteem, and be at peace in both mind and body.

Find something that you can always revert to to find peace whenever panic or anxiety hits you. Read positive books, watch self-improvement videos, and improve your personality and emotional stability.

Once you are more self-aware and capable of handling the wolves in the big bad world, you will be more than ready to handle whatever it can throw at you. It will also dissuade you from stalling from your new venture or quest of overcoming your shyness and making new friends.

## 3. Start small and keep it slow

Building new connections is not a race to the finish line. You are not competing with anyone (whether outside your circle or not), but yourself. You will always be the winner in the long run, no matter how much time it takes for you to finish and achieve your goals.

Since you will be a novice at making new friends, it is best to start slow and small. You can begin with the people you already know, such as friends, family, cousins, and other relatives.

If your friend is meeting up with his other friends that you do not know, get invited to the party. Your friend will be your shoulder to lean on in case you falter. Listen to others at the party and get to know them. If they are talking about something you like, you may offer your opinion on it whenever you get the chance. That will be the way in. After that, you have to make the effort to meet them more often and see where it leads to.

## 4. Online connections

We are living in the best of times, where we can forge friendships, reconnect with old friends, schoolmates, college friends, and ex-colleagues. You can find them on Facebook, LinkedIn, Twitter, and other social networking sites. Take the first step and contact them – ask them how they are doing and that you remember a specific positive part about them that has enriched you.

Once you get the engine rolling, you will learn on your own, and they will be delighted to reconnect with you. Two things are important – taking the first step and, listening or understanding what the other person is telling you; then your journey towards making friends and building new connections will be a smooth and joyful ride.

## The Limitations of Support and the Importance of Blooming from Within

No matter how well and lovingly a person helps you, the ultimate transformation must come from within. So, out of these four pillars that would endorse your growth, being at peace with yourself must be the prime one.

The famous words from Jim Kwik, "Great things always begin from the inside", that you see everywhere on social media are simple but extremely puissant. Once you start helping yourself, balancing your mind, and cherishing your soul, you will begin to feel more confident as a matter of course.

Building up self-confidence and finding the will to put it to optimum use is after all, what this venture out of shyness and social anxiety is all about.

# Chapter 8

## The Way Out into A New Vaster World

A whole new world, a new fantastic point of view". This song from Disney's classic movie Aladdin accurately demonstrates what is waiting for you on the other side. Social anxiety or shyness will no longer dictate your life experiences nor prevent you from going where you want to go. Remember to first identify and zero in on the exact issue you are facing as we discussed in chapter 1. It's no matter whether you are struggling with shyness, social anxiety, or both, the concepts in this book will help you.

Social anxiety may be difficult but it's not insurmountable. All you need is the will and desire to address your diffidence and fears. Once you have made up your mind to face the bullies, you will gain motivation and confidence.

For this, find whatever way that works for you. But, you can always seek help. When you invest more time and energy in fitness, reading, creative hobbies, journaling, and reflection, your life-goals will find you naturally. While working on new skills, daring to do new things, and helping others, always remember the value of being yourself. Conquering each step on your journey out of shyness and social anxiety must become your blissful reward.

Never forget that your achievements are yours alone; no one could have fought the battles you have fought so far. Value yourself, your space, your ideologies, and your self-esteem more than anything else because even when everything seemed lost, they were the only treasures that stuck by you.

I have discussed several different ways and techniques to overpower timidity. Since you are unique, customize these techniques to suit your needs and interests. Go back and refer to each chapter as many times as necessary. Of course, your sharp mind (that every shy person has) may have already decided your plan of action. But if you are a careful planner, it's time to pamper yourself with a new journal to plan it out, journal your achievements, study your failures, and get on your way. You can start by fixing in your mind that no matter how many times you may need to try, you will learn and do more. Along with that, be aware, maintain your peace, and keep a healthy self-esteem. Even if you fail, be cool about it. Don't sweat, don't fret, and on you will get!

I remember the day after I gave my speech to the large audience of students and teachers. It was my first real victory over social anxiety. Many more victories followed as I continued to grow and practice all the concepts that I have shared with you. I will forever be indebted to Mrs. Magalona who challenged me to step out of my comfort zone and thereby opening new doors of rich possibilities. I now challenge you to do the same and discover your new world today.

# NOTE TO READER

I'm so excited that you are on the journey to conquer shyness and social anxiety. If this book has helped you, consider writing a review to share your experience with other readers. Also, like my Facebook page (Reniel Anca - Author) to learn more tips from me

**Cheers!**

# REFERENCES

Baskerville, T., & Douglas, A. (2010). Dopamine and Oxytocin Interactions Underlying Behaviors: Potential Contributions to Behavioral Disorders. *CNS Neuroscience & Therapeutics, 16*(3), e92- e123.

Bernhardt, P., Dabbs Jr, J., Fielden, J., & Lutter, C. (1998). Testosterone changes during vicarious experiences of winning and losing among fans at sporting events. *Physiology & Behavior, 65*(1), 59-62.

Brown, K., & Ryan, R. (2003). The benefits of being present: Mindfulness and its role in psychological wellbeing. Journal Of Personality And Social Psychology, 84(4), 822-848.

Cain, S. (2013). Quiet: The Power Of Introverts in a World That Can't Stop Talking (1st ed.). Penguin Books.

Cash, T. (1984). The irrational beliefs test: Its relationship with cognitive-behavioral traits and depression. Journal Of Clinical Psychology, 40(6), 1399-1405.

Cheek, J., & Buss, A. (1981). Shyness and sociability. Journal Of Personality And Social Psychology, 41(2), 330-339.

Cuddy, A., Wilmuth, C., & Carney, D. (2012). The Benefit of Power Posing Before a High-Stakes Social Evaluation. Harvard

Business School Working Paper, No. 13-027. Retrieved 14 October 2020, from.

Edmondson, A. (2011). Strategies for learning from failure. Harvard Business Review, 89(4), 48-55.

Eisenberger, N., & Jarcho, J. (2006). An Experimental Study of Shared Sensitivity to Physical Pain and Social Rejection. Pain, 126(1-3), 132-138.

Eisenberger, N., Taylor, S., Gable, S., Hilmert, C., & Lieberman, M. (2007). Neural pathways link social support to attenuated neuroendocrine stress responses. Neuroimage, 35(4), 1601-1612.

Ekeland, E., Heian, F., Hagen, K., Abbott, J., & Nordheim, L. (2004). Exercise to improve self-esteem in children and young people. Cochrane Database Of Systematic Reviews.

Horn, J., Plomin, R., & Rosenman, R. (1976). Heritability of personality traits in adult male twins. Behavior Genetics, 6(1), 17-30.

Korb, A. (2015). The Upward Spiral. New Harbinger Publications.

Montoya, P., & Larbig, W. (2004). Influence of social support and emotional context on pain processing and magnetic brain responses in fibromyalgia. Arthritis And Rheumatology, 50(12), 4035–4044.

Pilkonis, P. (1977). The behavioral consequences of shyness. Journal Of Personality, 45(4), 596-611.

Ranganathan, V., Siemionow, V., Liu, J., Sahgal, V., & Yue, G. (2004). From mental power to muscle power—gaining strength by using the mind. Neuropsychologia, 42(7), 944-956.

Sani, S., Fathirezaie, Z., Brand, S., Pühse, U., Holsboer-Trachsler, E., Gerber, M., & Talepasand, S. (2016). Physical activity and self-esteem: testing direct and indirect relationships associated with psychological and physical mechanisms. Neuropsychiatric Disease And Treatment, Volume 12, 2617-2625.

Suda, M., Takei, Y., Aoyama, Y., Narita, K., Sato, T., Fukuda, M., & Mikuni, M. (2010). Frontopolar activation during face-to-face conversation: An in situ study using near-infrared spectroscopy. Neuropsychologia, 48(2), 441-447.

Uvnäs-Moberg, K. (1998). Oxytocin May Mediate The Benefits Of Positive Social Interaction And Emotions. Psychoneuroendocrinology, 23(8), 819-835

Walsh, J. (2002). Shyness and Social Phobia A Social Work Perspective on a Problem in Living. Health & Social Work, 27(2), 137-144.

Zeidan, F., Martucci, K., Kraft, R., McHaffie, J., & Coghill, R. (2013). Neural correlates of mindfulness meditation-related anxiety relief. Social Cognitive And Affective Neuroscience, 9(6), 751-759.

Manufactured by Amazon.ca
Bolton, ON